Nowadays

Jada Zenella

Presentation by *BookLeaf Publishing*

Web: www.bookleafpub.com

E-mail: info@bookleafpub.com

ISBN: 9789357212908

First edition 2023

This one is for you mom. May your soul shine upon this book as you rest in heaven. I miss you and love you.

ACKNOWLEDGEMENT

I don't think I'll be able to acknowledge everyone that helped in my lifetime but I pray all those that did know I am forever grateful to you.

Special thanks to
Byron Broussard (the photographer behind the cover art design on this book)
My sisters
My friends old and new.
All my teachers and mentors that got me to this point.
Thank you for being there for me always.

PREFACE

Jump with me
into pieces of myself.
Watch my words
take off like birds
flying into the sun.
I leave my heart
among the pages.

Nowadays

Nowadays I am simmering
down into all I manifested.
Yet I feel what lingers may be
my undoing on this plain.
I exist for many reasons.
You are one of them, many of them.
Who am I and who are you?
Nowadays I question myself
despite creating a life I want.
Nowadays I am satisfied with the surroundings
of my daily existence,
but fires are rising on the plain.
I am creating an essence of drama,
so I don't forget...

me

You
held me up above the stars,
so i could turn my eyes downward
towards the earth in hopes of seeing,
Seeing an identity i belong to outside of
You
did not care if i fell from that high.
You
mutilated my sense of being.
You
told me i had my place among the stars,
but only through your hands.
You
circle around me like a snake
closing me off to anything else besides
You
But without
You
i would be a different
me.

I am

I take measures to be what you want.
Like I'm on the hunt for a perfect me
wraped in a nice package in a big bow.
I don't know how to be me anymore.
My hardwire has been clipped and redone
to match yours.
But you're not here,
and I fear all my traits are bits of you scattered
in pieces of a past
I thought I escaped.
But, again, you're not here!
So I'm standing here screaming,
and is this me or is this you?
But, as I said before, you're not here...
But I am.

Present Moments

Backwards I screamed towards you.
"We did it! We survived!"
Every manic state of being that caused
ripples in our confidence, ripping
our soul a part, alone with every fight,
a fight to maintain our life in this world.
We did it though, we conquered every
breakdown and wild thought that crossed us.
We survived unimaginable turmoil
most of it created at our own hands,
a lot of it partiated by those we trusted most.
Now we stand before our success,
haunted by the past that created this
Present moment.

God and Anger

I have a distinct memory not of you,
A few distinct memories not of you,
but memories of your absence.
I climbed mountains of chaoactic memories
to beg you to climb back with me.
I do recall you being fearless
but not afraid to stay the same.
Funny like a fart in a middle classroom.
Femine in nature, masculine in rage.
You were not given what you needed,
and you provided me with what you knew.
You knew a cascade of useless facts.
You rambled we sort of listened.
I do not blame you but it often feels
God and anger were my only father.

November

Not every memory is a bear trap,
Opened wide for the last of the
Very moist stuffing your mom made.
Every chocolate cookie your aunt made.
Memories of your creepy uncle.
Buried deep the laughter of your family.
Evening naps among the house we laid.
Ready for next year...

Abstract

Absence of images created by words,
but present in original voice and mood.
Satisfaction in the form of simplicity.
Tactfully in place with all wordy aspects.
Reasons being to make me better.
Are you acting like a Mary?
Can you understand outside your old voice?
Trying to let it go.

Pour Out

I set myself on fire...
The smoke rose higher,
a blazing flame engulfing me.
I frantically run to the sea.
I try to soothe the burns,
but I have to wait my turn.
The blisters begin to swell.
My heart begin to pour out,
I fell deep into the ocean blue.

Attractive Song

I am playing a game
of where's Waldo with my inner self.
Trying to repair the damage.
Trying to seal off the busted pipes,
The caved in emotions that wrap
around my reality becoming
the center of the distressed,
the mess that is me...
I am missing something...
I peep through windows with no glass
waiting for all my tortured days to pass.
And I could describe my tears like rain,
or anger like thunder but nothing feels
real anymore, so I will eat my meals
alone, and with others trying to convince
myself that nothing is wrong,
but that is not an attractive song.

I weep

I haven't shaken like this in a while,
and although my mind will lie to me
in all honesty it sounds like the truth.
"Everyone hates you!" My mind whispers.
The wind is blowing. The sun is out.
And tears rush down my face because
the world despises my very existence
and I weep.

Whoah is me

The people I admire most
are those with the ability
to stay calm, collective, and private.
Those professional type people
but I am never able to maintain that.

Instead I just leak like a faucet
from my eyes at all hours,
day and night!

I wallow in the fields of misery
contructed from tarnished dreams
and open bleeding memories that
unfortunately never properly healed

Pieces

To heal is to dig up that deep hole
and pull out every bloody mangled
piece of yourself you cut up long ago.
Pieces you buried in the dead of night.
"No one must know." You would whisper.
You sliced and diced every thorn'd emotion
and threw it into a your own deep dark hole.
Parts of yourself screamed,
"Wait, don't do this." but you dissolve
into a mound of obsessive impulses
driven by a desire to be whole again...
Pieces can be pretty too, though.

Days yet to come

If in moments I faulter
Lift me up above the sky
to see what I cannot see.
To love what is hidden
among the noise, I shall rise,
for treasures I was made from
treasures I do have now,
even if the days are expansive,
Dark days digging to see the light,
I shall rise above the clouds
to thank the heavens for the days
dimmed with anxious electricity
Moments of being alive ready
to see days yet to come.

Okay

My favorite thing you did
was say, "You're okay."
Moments before I said
I'm sorry for the 100th
time in a row, but you
knew what really scared me
was the long silence between
conversations that allowed me
to second guess every word out
of my mouth and judge every
hand gesture I had made in front
of others, but you smiled at me,
and before the silence hit you said,
"You're okay."

Melt

If I spend too much time
alone with my thoughts
I start to bury myself
in non-existent turmoil.
My mind will latch
onto anything that will
bring tears to my eyes
and make my heart melt.

The Wave Remains

I thought maybe all of it would disappear.
That all the pain I feel or have felt
would somehow evaporate into the air.
That all anguish and uncertainty would simply
Go away...
I pour fresh boiled tea into an old mug,
I look around at the space I fought so hard
to create and to manifest
I can't help but feel...
I feel everything deeply;
I'm like a surgeon of emotions
Cutting myself open
Removing the tumor that grew inside me,
but I fear the cut is too deep to bandage up,
and my hope is I can keep the stitches
in their place before another wave
pulls them apart.

The wave remains

I live today

I live for today,
 because tomorrow
 may never come.
 I may never get
 the chance to
 climb the tallest
 snow covered mountain
 or travel lands of
 endless beauty.
 I may never drink
 the finest wine
 or taste
 the richest food.
 The black smoke from
 The White House chimney
 may never be clear,
 and my heart may,
 never settle--
 But I live today...
 I breathe today...
 I feel
 my lungs expand,
 and isn't it
 marvelous!
 Isn't it absolutely

amazing!
Isn't it truly
a blessing--
Just to be alive today...

Enough is enough

Sometimes I fight sleep.
I'm scared I'll miss something.
Even more so I feel
as if I'm not doing enough.
I'm not writing enough.
I'm not saving enough money.
I feel rest is for those
that have accomplished something.
I feel like my life has been
one long drag of a cigarette
and at any moment
I'll be put out and kicked to the curve.
And others will say she didn't do enough.
She wasn't enough.
Those other people don't exist
it's just me feeling like I'm not enough
like I'm washable chalk on the sidewalk
of an elementary school.
When will I feel like enough is enough?

Future

For I for saw the future;
Our bodies woven in red,
nestled tight in our beds.
Late in the night we woke
stirred by voices that spoke.
The practice of hatred spun
in a war we have yet won;
but around every heart
stamped a pivotal part
of wrongly painted skin
when all colors are friends,
and all brave women talk
when one is being stalked.
All those sparks of madness
with heavy silhouettes of sadness
drowning out the march of feet
dancing frantically in the streets.

Creaking and Cracking

Pave the way out for hope;
Hope that flutters
like your eyelashes.
If you blink you will miss all
Those fireworks going off,
the sound of a baby
crying in the distance,
and a mother running away.
Sacrifice and tears
swim around the family
Growing with your bones,
creaking and cracking

Things

There are so many things
I wish to say to others,
but I put it in a cave.
I cast it into darkness...